Pressure Point K
Made Easy

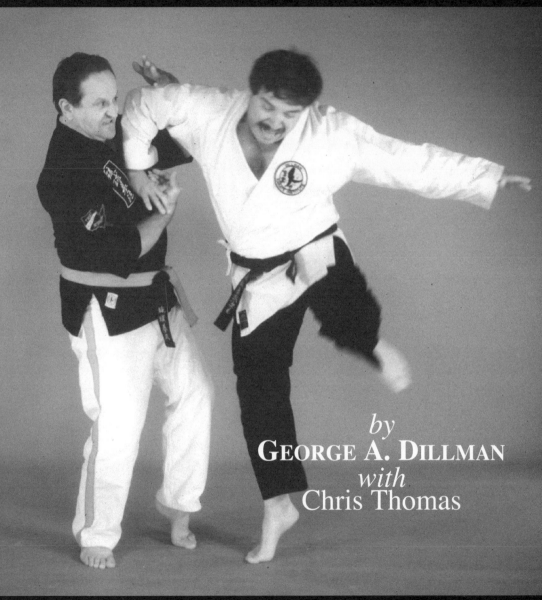

by
GEORGE A. DILLMAN
with
Chris Thomas

A guide to the **DILLMAN PRESSURE POINT METHOD**
for Beginners and Younger Martial Artists

A Dillman Karate International Book

First published in 1999 by:
Dillman Karate International, Publishers
251 Mt. View Rd, (Grill)
Reading, PA 19607
USA
www.dillman.com

Copyright 1999 Dillman Karate International
All rights reserved
First edition, 1999
Second printing, 2002
Library of Congress Catalog Card Number: 97-068274
ISBN 1-889267-02-3

15,000 copies in print

A NOTE TO THE READER

This book is written as a means of preserving a vital, historical aspect of the martial arts. Dillman Karate International, Publishers, and the authors make no representation, warranty or guarantee that the techniques described and illustrated in this book will be effective or safe in any self-defense situation or otherwise. You may be injured, or you may injure someone else if you train in the techniques presented within. We therefore suggest that you practice only under the supervision of a qualified instructor and exercise the utmost restraint in training. Dillman Karate International, Publishers, and the authors are in no way responsible for any injuries which may result from the practice or use of the techniques presented within. Some self-defense applications illustrated may not be justified in some circumstances under applicable federal, state or local law. Neither Dillman Karate International, Publishers, nor the authors make any representation or warranty regarding the legal or ethical appropriateness of any technique mentioned in this book.

ACKNOWLEDGEMENTS:

We would like to gratefully acknowledge the many people who have made this book possible. Our thanks to Wendy & Tom Countryman for principle photography, artwork, and for layout. Thanks to those who appear in the photos: Bill Burch, Adam Caswell, April Countryman, Josh Countryman, and Bruce Fronk. Special thanks to Kim Dillman for proof-reading and editorial advice. Our on-going thanks to our teachers, students and colleagues who continue to inspire us to new heights of knowledge and discovery.

DEDICATION

This book is dedicated to young martial artists everywhere:
You are the future.

157 black belts came from all over to attend the grand opening of George Dillman's new school in Reading, PA, on November 23, 1991. Some of them, including Professor Remy Presas, and Professor Wally Jay, are shown here.

Some of Dillman Karate International's senior instructors. Back row -- Will Higginbotham, George Dillman, Bob Golden, Greg Dillon, Chris Thomas. Front row -- Mickey Wittekiend, Dave Wilson, Bill Homann.

George and Kim Dillman with Maria, Elaine, Louise and Kim McMenamin at Grianan of Aileach, "Stone Ring Fort," in County Donegal, Ireland.

George Dillman is invited all over the world to teach his pressure point method. Here he is seen in Europe giving a seminar for a group of eager martial artists.

George Dillman appeared in the movie **TC 2000** with action stars Bolo Yeung and Billy Blanks. Yeung played a villain who fought Bruce Lee in **ENTER THE DRAGON**.

David Carradine and George Dillman exchange copies of their books at a martial arts store in Canada. Carradine is the star of the TV series **KUNG FU** and **KUNG FU: THE LEGEND CONTINUES**.

Benny "The Jet" Urquidez, and George Dillman pose with two young martial artists at a 1997 Dillman seminar. Urquidez is a world famous kick-boxer, and appeared in the film **GROSSE POINT BLANK**.

George Dillman, Harry G. Smith, and Chris Thomas. Smith was George Dillman's first karate sensei (teacher), and a direct student of Tatsuo Shimabuku, the founder of the Isshin-ryu style of karate.

In 1997, medical research was done at an east coast university hospital to look at pressure point techniques. Evidence from the study suggests that the Dillman Pressure Point Method can be used in self-defense without causing undue harm to an attacker. Here, Kim Dillman does a move on subject Bill Burch, with Dr. Chas Terry and Mark Kline assisting.

Caution:

Even though this book is for beginners and younger martial artists, the methods we show are effective and can cause injury.

Study Dillman Pressure Point Method only under the careful supervision of a qualified teacher. Do not try to learn it on your own.

TABLE OF CONTENTS

NOTE FOR PARENTS, EDUCATORS AND YOUNG MARTIAL ARTISTS

Around the turn of the twentieth century a revolution occurred in the martial art of karate. This once secret self-defense science was taught openly to school children as a form of physical education. In order for this to happen, it was necessary to water-down the art so that the students would not injure each other. This "children's karate" eventually spread around the world. As a result, virtually every karate school in this country teaches some version of the children's style.

"Children's karate" is known as **karate-do**. **Karate-do** is designed to teach discipline and control, as well as a competitive sport. But, it is not intended to teach genuine self-defense skills.

In this book, however, we present information on **karate-jitsu**. **Karate-jitsu** is the original method, undiluted for children. It is a self-defense art which has no game or sporting element. And while it does instill the values of self-control and discipline, its approach is very serious. This is self-protection, pure and simple.

Some may question the wisdom of presenting real self-defense techniques to young people. Wouldn't it be better to teach them the watered-down version, at least until they get older? This might be true if we knew that the young have no need for genuine self-defense, but, sadly, that is not the case.

The young men and women who are attracted to karate training tend to be intelligent and thoughtful individuals. These are the very same people who often find themselves the focus of a bully's unwelcome attention.

Bullies are seeking to wield power over others. Their tools are intimidation and violence. But bullies are mostly lazy. If a potential victim takes too much work to abuse, the bully will tend to look elsewhere. Even a smaller child, who is out-matched physically, can become too much of a bother to bully, provided he or she possesses some genuine fighting skills.

Here is an unfortunate truth. Sometime during seventh or eighth grade, a boy will probably be physically assaulted by a classmate. His response to the assault will in many ways determine what happens to him until he graduates from high school.

If he fights back courageously and decisively, he will gain a reputation as "someone not to be messed with" (regardless of the outcome of the confrontation). As a result, he will probably never have to fight again. If he is cowed by the attack, and helpless to respond, he will most certainly be subjected to repeated abuse in the future. His only recourse then will be to involve parents and teachers. And, while this is the course of action which adults usually recommend, it does not work. Adults cannot protect a boy from his peers. And if those peers label him as a "squealer," they will retaliate.

Sometime in seventh or eighth grade, a girl will probably be the object of sexually inappropriate behavior by the boys in her grade. This behavior may even go so far as physical assault (such as being groped by those boys). If she protects the integrity of her body decisively and courageously, her physical boundaries will be respected.

If, however, she is unable to act in self-protection, she will feel like a helpless victim. If she enlists the aid of parents and teachers, she will find that, while they are on her side, they are largely unable to truly protect her.

Most distressing of all is that children are assaulted by adults everyday. In these cases nothing but genuine and serious self-defense methods can offer any chance of escape.

It is because of considerations such as these that we have chosen to present this book. The material in this book is effective, and that is precisely what genuine self-protection requires.

Since this is the case, it becomes especially important that young martial artists are provided with moral guidance. Here are some suggestions to insure that serious martial arts are learned in a proper moral climate.

1. A karate student should make church, mosque, temple or synagogue attendance a regular part of his or her training. Parents can assist in this by attending right alongside their martial arts offspring.

2. A karate student should contemplate and discuss the ethical implications of karate techniques. Self-defense techniques can have serious consequences which must be anticipated in advance.

3. Observe the karate classes at a potential school before enrolling your child there. Make sure that the art is taught in a disciplined and respectful manner.

4. Understand that everyone has a right to protect themselves, and has a moral obligation to respect others.

5. Understand that no one deserves to be assaulted by another, and that when a self-defense response is required by circumstances, a person should only use as much force as is necessary to stop the threat and escape safely.

Carolina Sargent, age 13, Larry Sargent 5th degree black belt, Samantha Sargent, age 12. This photo was taken shortly after Carolina and Samantha earned their black belts.

"You want to *be* a black belt, but are you willing to *become* a black belt?"

CHAPTER ONE: The History of Karate

Our art of karate comes from **Okinawa**. Okinawa is an island between Japan and China. A long time ago it was illegal for the people of Okinawa to carry any kind of weapon. At first, this rule was made by an Okinawan king named Shoshin. Then, in 1609, Japanese samurai invaded Okinawa and took over. The Japanese did not let the Okinawan people carry weapons either. With the samurai soldiers around, the people of Okinawa did not feel safe. So, they wanted to know how to fight.

During that time, people from China lived in Okinawa. Some of them knew **kempo**, the Chinese art of fighting. The Chinese taught kempo to the Okinawans. The Okinawans also had their own fighting art called **te**. They mixed kempo with te and made a new art called **Ryukyu kempo karate-jitsu**.

The word *Ryukyu* means "Okinawa." The word *kempo* means "boxing." The word *kara* means "China." The word *te* means "hand." The word *jitsu* means "fighting art." So, *Ryukyu kempo karate-jitsu* means, "Okinawan boxing, Chinese-hand fighting art." Because this is such a long name, it is mostly just called kempo or karate.

The study of weapons was also a part of karate. Since it was illegal for people to own weapons, the karate experts had to use farming and fishing tools. They were very good at fighting with wooden poles, boat oars and hand-tools.

Things started to change about 1860. At that time, Japan stopped having samurai soldiers, and built an army like the armies of Russia and the United States. The new army used guns and cannons, so no one cared if the Okinawan people learned self-defense, or learned to use poles and oars as weapons.

In 1902 a karate master named **Itosu** started to teach karate to school children. For the first time, karate was taught in public, and not in secret. Itosu changed the karate he taught the children so that it would not be so dangerous. He wanted the children to learn self-control and fitness. He thought it was more important for them to be good people than to be good fighters.

One of Itosu's students was a man named **Funakoshi**. Funakoshi went around with some of his friends to show people what karate was all about. Once he was asked to show karate to the Japanese prince. This was in 1922. The prince and the people with him were very pleased with karate. They asked Funakoshi to come to Japan to show this art. There he found that the Japanese people were eager to learn karate. So, he stayed in Japan the rest of his life to teach.

Funakoshi agreed with Itosu's ideas about karate, and he taught, "The goal of karate is not winning and losing; it is to be a better person inside." Itosu had wanted a new name for karate so that everyone would know that it was not just about fighting. So he used different words to make the name karate. Instead of writing **karate-jitsu**, "Chinese hand fighting method," he wrote, **karate-do**, which means, "the way of the empty hand." Funakoshi helped spread this idea, and was one of the first people to write **karate-do** the new way.

The new name was trying to say that karate training is a way to empty our hearts of what is mean and bad. Many other karate teachers liked this idea and followed Funakoshi's lead. They began to use the name **karate-do** and teach the way Itosu taught the school children.

In Okinawa, some of the old masters worried that karate was becoming a weak art, so they kept the name **karate-jitsu** and taught the old karate, which is used for fighting. They also taught the old way, keeping their **karate-jitsu** secret.

Even today there are still these same two ideas about karate. Some people think it is for self-control, fitness, and to be a better person. Other people think that karate is for fighting and self-defense.

The people who teach the older, more dangerous **karate-jitsu** do not teach very many people. This is out of fear that someone might learn from them and then try to hurt others. But, the people who teach **karate-do** will teach most anybody. They think that good karate makes for a

good person. For this reason, **karate-do** is practiced all over the world, and **karate-jitsu** is still mostly a secret.

The style of karate in this book is called **Ryukyu kempo Tomari-te**. This is a very old type of **karate-jitsu**. It is named for a small village on Okinawa called Tomari, where it came from. Though the book is about this one style, the ideas will work with any style.

Ryukyu kempo Tomari-te is for self-defense. Everyone should try to be a better person. And **karate-jitsu** can teach us how to be good people just like **karate-do** can. You should want to be a good person. But, the best place to learn this is your church, mosque, temple or synagogue. A dojo (karate school) is a place to learn self-defense.

We are not afraid that people will use this art for hurting others, because **karate-jitsu** takes many years to learn. People who only want to hurt others will just grab a knife, or get a gun. And we are not afraid to teach fighting secrets to young people. Everyday, young people are attacked and hurt. Training in either **karate-do** or **karate-jitsu** can help a person to be brave and strong. But only in **karate-jitsu** can a person learn real skills in self-defense.

KARATE STYLES

Karate was created on Okinawa by combining Chinese fighting arts, Okinawan fighting arts, and Japanese fighting arts. Today we call the Chinese fighting arts **kung fu**. But, it was not called kung fu in the old days, it was called **chuan fa**. Chuan fa means "fist method" or "boxing". In Okinawan speech, chuan fa is pronounced **kempo**.

Many years ago there where only three types of karate. They were called **Naha-te**, **Shuri-te** and **Tomari-te**. The word te means hand. Naha and Shuri are cities on Okinawa, and Tomari is a village. These were the three main places karate came from. Once karate was taught in public, teachers began to share ideas, and new styles were created. Today, there are many kinds of karate.

The different kinds are called **ryu**, which means "style." Each style has its own way of doing the art, and its own ideas about what is most important to learn. Some ryu are **karate-jitsu**, some are **karate-do** and some are a mix of both. Also, the Japanese people made some changes to karate. This means that the karate in Japan is not the same as the karate in Okinawa.

Karate masters gave names to their styles. These names say something about the style. **Goju-ryu** means, "Hard/soft style." The name tells the main idea the style is based on. **Shorin-ryu** means "Pine forest style." "Pine forest" is the name of a Chinese temple where kempo was taught. The name Shorin-ryu is in honor of the Chinese part of karate.

Here is a list of some of the main styles of karate.

OKINAWAN KARATE STYLES

```
Goju-ryu ─────────┐
Uechi-ryu ────────┼───── NAHA-TE
Ryuei-ryu ────────┘
Isshin-ryu
Matsumura Shorin-ryu ──┐
Shobayashi Shorin-ryu ─┼───── SHURI-TE
Kobayashi Shorin-ryu ──┘
Motobu-ryu
Shorinji-ryu
Shorei-ryu ────────────┐
                       ├───── TOMARI-TE
Ryukyu Kempo Tomari-te ┘
```

JAPANESE KARATE STYLES

Shotokan-ryu
Wado-ryu
Goju-kai
Kyokushinkai

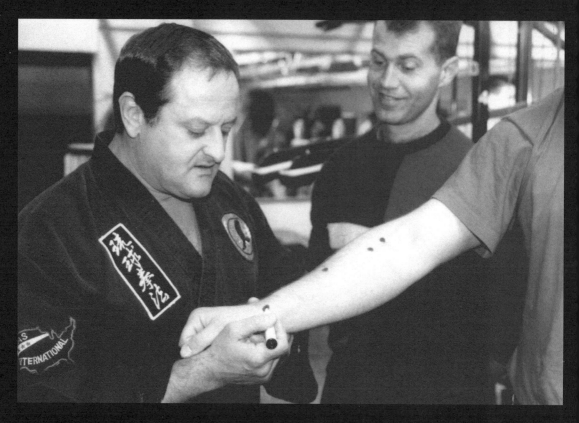

Author George Dillman teaching the location of arm pressure points to eager students at a seminar on the Dillman Method.

"The three most important secrets of karate are, practice, practice, practice. (The fourth is, always use pressure points.)"

CHAPTER TWO: The Pressure Points
(KYUSHO)

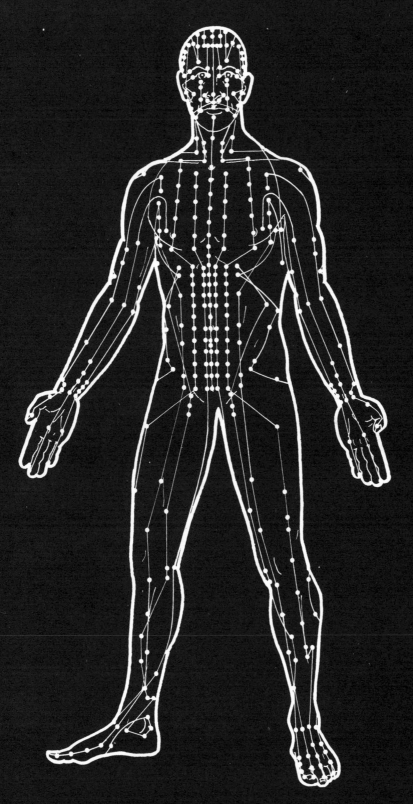

Before we talk about the moves of **karate-jitsu**, we must talk about the main idea. This is the heart of real karate: using pressure points. Everyone knows that the body has spots that are easy to hurt. A poke in the eye can end a fight. So can a punch in the stomach. These places are called **vital targets**.

But, **karate-jitsu** uses spots that are not well known, spots that can end a fight very easily. These spots are called **pressure points** or **kyusho** (sounds like *cue-show*). Pressure points are used in a healing art called **acupuncture**. In this art, a doctor will stick a fine needle into a pressure point to help a sick person get better. It may sound strange, but acupuncture works and has been used for over 5,000 years.

The idea in acupuncture is that life force, or **ki**, must be balanced in the body. When a part of the body has too much or too little ki it can cause an illness. Ki runs through the body along paths called **meridians**. Pressure points are spots on the paths where the doctor can speed up, or slow down the ki.

In **karate-jitsu**, these same pressure points are touched, or rubbed, or hit to stop the ki. When the ki stops, a person becomes weak and cannot fight. It does not take strength to do this, but it does take skill.

Each pressure point has a name, but we do not use those names. Instead, we use the point numbers found in acupuncture books. Each path is named after an organ of the body and each point is numbered in order on the path. So, Lung # 5, or L-5, is the fifth point on the lung path. When you are first learning about the points,

Mark Kline uses a light hit to pressure points to make a volunteer faint. This is very advanced, and should only be tried by experts.

you will mix up the numbers. Later it gets easier to remember.

There is a game called *paper-scissors-rock*. In this game, you and a friend show either an open hand (*paper*), two fingers (*scissors*) or a fist (*rock*). If you show *paper*, and your friend shows *rock*, you win, because, "*Paper covers rock.*" But, if your friend shows *scissors*, you lose, because, "*Scissors cut paper.*" And, if your friend had *scissors*, but you chose *rock*, you would be the winner. "*Rock smashes scissors.*"

In pressure point fighting, or **kyusho-jitsu** (sounds like *cue-show-jit-soo*), there are five things that act like paper-scissors-rock, called the **five elements**. They are, *Metal*, *Wood*, *Earth*, *Water*, and *Fire*. Now, it is not real metal, or real wood. It is just that it is like metal or wood in some way.

In kyusho-jitsu, *Metal* cuts *Wood*, *Wood* enters *Earth*, *Earth* holds *Water*, *Water* puts out *Fire* and *Fire* melts *Metal*. Each follows in order. In fighting, we might start by attacking a *Wood* point, then hit an *Earth* point. Since *Wood* enters *Earth*, the *Earth* point is made weak. Next, because *Earth* holds *Water*, our next attack would be to a *Water* point. This will make the person weak, and the fight will be over.

The moves we show in this book use points in the right order for fighting. You do not need to know why they follow the order we show. Just learn to do them.

There are over 350 pressure points on the body. In **karate-jitsu** we use about 1/3 of these for self-defense. Still, it is hard to learn over 100 points all at once. So, we always start by teaching a few very important points on the arms and legs. You must learn these points well if you want to progress in the art.

When you are a more advanced karate student, you will want to study more about the pressure points in our books, **KYUSHO-JITSU: The Dillman Method of Pressure Point Fighting**, **Advanced Pressure Point Fighting of RYUKYU KEMPO** and **Advanced Pressure Point Grappling— TUITE**.

Now this is important, ***NEVER, EVER HIT A PRESSURE POINT ON SOMEONE!!!!!*** Your **karate-jitsu** teacher may have you learn to hit points on the arm, but, you should never do it by yourself. If your teacher knows real **karate-jitsu**, then he or she will know how to teach you safely.

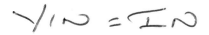

The Pressure Points
THE INNER ARM

Lung # 8, L-8

WHERE IT IS: On the inside of the wrist, where a nurse takes your pulse.

HOW IT WORKS: Squeeze or rub towards the hand. It will make a fist open up.

Heart # 6, H-6

WHERE IT IS: 1/2" from the crease of the wrist on the inside of the arm, along the bottom edge.

HOW IT WORKS: Press or touch into the small bone of your wrist. It makes the wrist bend.

Lung # 6, L-6

WHERE IT IS: On the inside of the arm, along the top edge, halfway between the elbow and the wrist.

HOW IT WORKS: Hit towards the hand. It will make the fist weak.

Extra Point: M-UE-28

WHERE IT IS: On the inside of the arm, along the bottom edge, halfway between the elbow and wrist.

HOW IT WORKS: Hit to make the wrist bend and the hand open.

Lung # 5, L-5

WHERE IT IS: At the bend of the elbow on the inside of the arm, near the top edge.

HOW IT WORKS: Hit with a hooking blow to bend the arm.

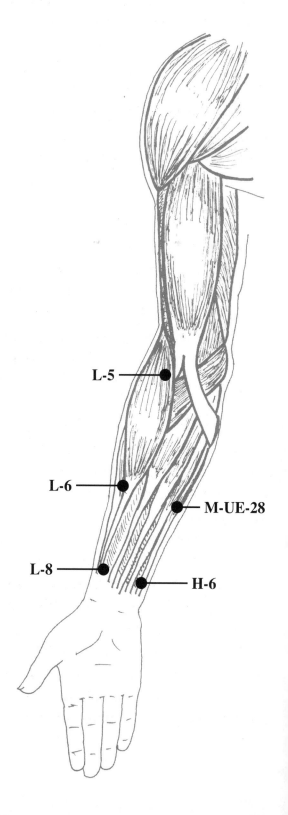

YANG - R OUT

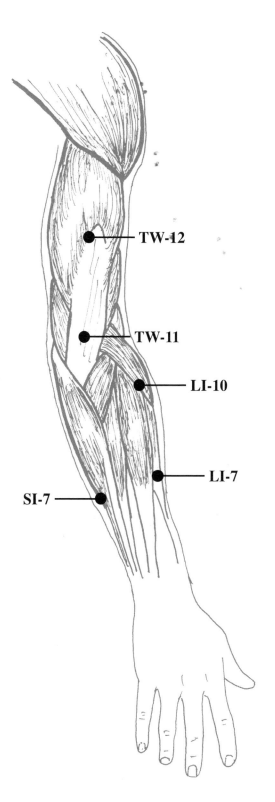

TW-12

TW-11

LI-10

LI-7

SI-7

THE OUTER ARM

Large Intestine # 7, LI-7

WHERE IT IS: On outside of the arm, along the top edge, halfway between the elbow and the wrist.

HOW IT WORKS: Strike towards the hand to weaken the arm.

Small Intestine # 7, SI-7

WHERE IT IS: On the outside of the arm, at the bottom edge, halfway between the elbow and wrist.

HOW IT WORKS: Strike into the center of the forearm to weaken the arm.

Large Intestine # 10, LI-10

WHERE IT IS: Between the muscles, just outside of the crease of the elbow.

HOW IT WORKS: Hit this point down towards the bone to cramp the arm.

Triple Warmer # 11, TW-11

WHERE IT IS: On the back of the arm, just above the point of the elbow.

HOW IT WORKS: Rub up and down to straighten the arm.

Triple Warmer # 12, TW-12

WHERE IT IS: On the back of the arm in the middle of the muscle (triceps).

HOW IT WORKS: Hit this point towards the bone to throw the shoulder and straighten the arm.

THE LOWER BODY

Ki-Center
(Conception # 3,4,5,6, Co-3,4,5,6)

WHERE IT IS: On the lower stomach, about three inches below the belly button. This is the center of internal energy (ki).

HOW IT WORKS: Hit to fold the body and sap strength from an attacker.

Spleen # 12, Sp-12

WHERE IT IS: At the crease where your thigh joins your hip.

HOW IT WORKS: Hit to bend the body over.

Spleen # 11, Sp-11

WHERE IT IS: In the middle of the inner thigh.

HOW IT WORKS: Hit at an outward angle to buckle the leg.

Spleen # 10, Sp-10

WHERE IT IS: Above and inside the knee.

HOW IT WORKS: Hit at an angle, down and out, to buckle the knee.

LI 20 - SIDE o
NOS

LI 19

LI 19

LI

L 2

STOMAC
5

LI
18
SIDE
N

STOM 17

L 3

L 4

STOM 18

L 5

Co-6
Co-5
Co-4
Co-3

Sp-12

Sp-11

Sp-10

Sp6

In the photos above, George Dillman is using a kick to Sp-11 to stop one attacker, while using wrist points and joint turning (tuite) to deal with a second opponent. Notice how the kick to Sp-11 causes the attacker's ankle to buckle (circled), knocking him to the ground.

Even though **Remy Presas**, **George Dillman** and **Wally Jay** are three of the most respected and sought-after martial arts teachers in the world today, they still work to improve their skills. For them, martial arts is a lifetime study.

"Real masters don't brag about how much they know. They are too busy learning more"

CHAPTER THREE: Karate Stances
(TACHI-WAZA)

Stances are special ways to stand when fighting. Stances can be either short or long. Short stances are better for moving quickly. Long stances are better for energy transfer. Short stances are good when hitting pressure points. Long stances are good when twisting joints. Which stance you use in self-defense depends on what you are doing. So, it is good to learn both types.

FRONT STANCE *(ZENKUTSU-DACHI)*:

Bend one leg in front, over the foot. Set the other leg back, almost straight. Do not lock the back leg. There is more weight on the front leg. This stance is used to put energy to the front.

HORSE STANCE (*KIBA-DACHI*):

Spread the feet wide, and bend the knees. It looks like you are riding a horse. This stance puts energy down, or to the sides.

CAT STANCE *(NEKO-DACHI)*:

Bend one leg and put most of your weight on it. Slide the other leg one step forward, with the heel raised and the ball of the foot touching the ground. This stance covers the legs and groin from attack.

"**G**reatness is measured by how you treat those who are weaker than yourself."

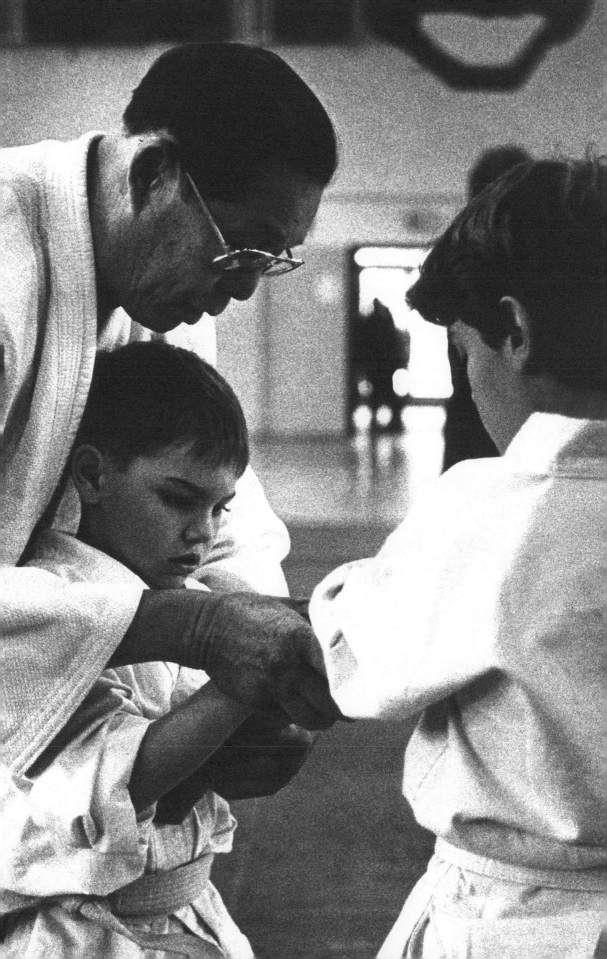

Young karate students training at the Dillman Karate
International main dojo
(school) in Reading, PA.

CHAPTER FOUR: Hand Skills
(TE-WAZA)

Every basic move has many uses. We will show a simple way to use each one. But don't think that simple is bad. The best way to defend yourself is to use simple moves that really work.

In this book we will teach you to use *"two points of contact."* This means that with each move you will touch, hit, or grab the attacker in two places. You will mostly use one hand at a time. If you keep studying **karate-jitsu**, you will learn to use both hands at the same time.

Each basic move of **karate-jitsu** can end a fight by itself. But, if it doesn't, you must be ready with a follow-up move.

"When you reach black belt, you are finally a beginner."

BASIC PUNCH *(TSUKI)*:

Begin with your right fist at the hip, palm up, and your left fist out. Punch the right fist straight forward, and twist it, while you pull your left fist to your hip. (1-3)

The punch does not go to the very center, but a little to the side. Also, the fist turns only part way around, ending at an angle. At the end of the punch, the wrist tips forward. This type of punch is the best for fighting.

STEP-PUNCH *(OI-ZUKI)*:

If you step forward with your left foot and punch with your left fist (or you step with your right foot and punch with your right fist) it is called a step punch. (4)

REVERSE-PUNCH *(GYAKU-ZUKI)*:

If your left foot is forward and you punch with your right hand (or your right foot is forward and you punch with your left hand) it is called a reverse punch. (5)

USING THE BASIC PUNCH:

1. An attacker is about to punch you. He has his right foot forward. You are standing with your feet apart and your hands at your side.

2-3. Step forward with your left foot, and step on his right foot.

4-5. Shift your weight onto your left leg to take a front stance. At the same time, punch his chest with your left hand.

Notice that you are using a long front stance. This big stance helps you to strongly pin your attacker's foot. It also allows you to direct your strength into your punch.

"Your punch must be fast, like a cowboy drawing his gun. As your attacker reacts to being hit, he will fall back. Because you are on his foot, he will lose his balance and fall over. He may even hurt his ankle."

DOWNWARD COUNTER *(GEDAN-UKE)*:

Reach one fist up near the face, and bring the other forward. Swing the one fist down over your leg and pull the other fist to your hip.

"Counter moves *(uke-waza)* are very important in **karate-jitsu**. They are used to stop a fight quickly. In **karate-do** these moves are called blocks, but this is wrong. School-children were told this so they would not hurt each other."

USING THE DOWNWARD COUNTER:

1-2. As an attacker reaches for you, grab the index finger of his right hand with your right hand.

3-4. Bend his finger back as you turn your right palm up, and bring your hand up near your face.

4-6. Sweep your hand down, and drive your attacker to the floor. (Quickly escape by running away.)

DETAILED EXPLANATION

When you grab the attacker's finger, you must first bend it back and down [A,B]. Then, with a scooping motion, swing his finger up towards your face [C,D,E].

Use a scooping motion again to bring the attacker to the ground as you complete the downward counter movement [E,F,G,H].

MIDDLE COUNTER *(CHUDAN-UKE)*:

First, bring one hand across the body, and hold the other hand up in front of the face. Then swing the first hand out and to the front. At the same time, pull the other hand down to the hip.

USING THE MIDDLE COUNTER:

1. An attacker grabs your right arm with his right hand.

2. Do the middle counter motion so that you trap his hand in the bend of your elbow. (The secret is to squeeze his little finger so it folds over his ring finger.)

3-4. Take a step forward with your left foot, then turn to your right. As you make your turn, the pressure on your attacker's fingers and wrist will drive him away from you. This gives you a chance to quickly escape.

Notice that you are using a short front stance. We said that short stances were good for moving quickly. Since this move depends on the actions of stepping and turning, we use the short stance.

(This use of the middle counter, and the use we have shown for the downward counter, are examples of the art of **Tuite***, or "joint turning." To find out more about this art, see our book,* **Advanced Pressure Point Grappling — TUITE***.)*

UPWARD COUNTER *(AGE-UKE):*

Bring one fist across your body, and the other up in front. Swing the one fist up in front of your forehead and pull the other fist to your hip.

66**I**f you want to master Ryukyu kempo, you must first master your temper."

USING THE UPWARD COUNTER:

1. An attacker has grabbed you with his left hand and is ready to punch with his right. You are standing with your hands up, saying, "I don't want to fight." Only if you are certain he intends to punch you do you continue.

2-3. With your right hand, pin his fist to your body so that he cannot let go of you. Hit his left arm with your left fist at LI-10 near his elbow.

4-6. Drive your left forearm up into his jaw, while you continue to trap his hand at your chest.

NOTE: All of the advanced moves of **karate-jitsu** *use both hands at the same time. This basic move gives a taste of what lies ahead.*

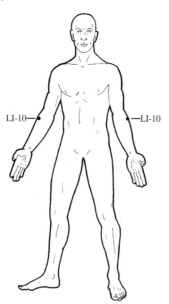

Martial Arts Morality: If you are attacked as shown here, you are in danger. Your attacker can hit you repeatedly in the face and cause you severe harm. This use of the upward counter can cause injury to your attacker. You should only use this move if:

1) You believe that your attacker actually intends to hit you, rather than just scare you.
2) You cannot find a non-violent way to protect yourself.

KNIFE-HAND COUNTER *(SHUTO-UKE)*:

Bring one open hand across your face, and extend the other open hand forward. Chop outward with the one hand, and draw the other near your stomach.

USING THE KNIFE HAND COUNTER:

1. An enemy is about to hit you. Stand with your feet apart, and your hands up near your shoulders. Tell him, "I don't want to fight."

2-3. He throws a left punch at your head. With your left hand, chop his arm halfway between elbow and wrist at L-6.

4-5. Step forward into a left front stance and chop to his neck with your left open hand.

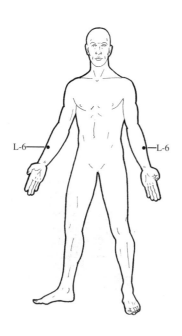

"Be ready to stop yourself. When you chop your attacker's arm, it may end the fight. Do not finish the move and strike his neck unless you have no other choice."

M artial artists from other systems of karate come to seminars on the Dillman Pressure Point Method in order to learn some of the very same things we show in this book.

At a seminar taught by co-author Chris Thomas, a third-degree black belt in Japanese-style karate practices the same use of upward counter that is shown on pages 52-53.

CHAPTER FIVE: Kicking Skills
(KERI-WAZA)

Karate-do is famous for its many kicking skills. The kicks of **karate-jitsu** are not as flashy, but they are more useful. If your goal is to be a stunt-actor and do fights for movies, you should work on **karate-do** kicks. If you want to be able to protect yourself, use **karate-jitsu**.

FRONT KICK *(MAE-GERI)*:

Lift your knee with your leg bent, and pull the toes up tight. Swing your leg out and drive the ball of the foot forward. Then recoil the kick by pulling the foot back. The kick snaps out and back like a whip.

USING THE FRONT KICK:

1-3. An attacker punches at your face with his right hand. Brush his punch to your right with your left hand. Bring your right arm up along the outside of his arm.

4. With your right hand, grab his wrist, squeezing the pressure points H-6 and L-8.

5-6. Pull his arm to your hip and kick him between his belt and his groin — the ki-center — with your right front kick.
Note: Methods for catching a punch are detailed in **KYUSHO-JITSU: The Dillman Method of Pressure Point Fighting**, *pgs 259-267.*

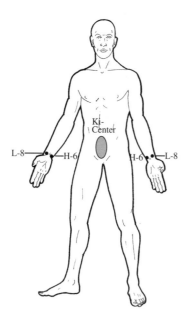

INSIDE KICK *(NAIHANCHI-GERI)*:

Raise the leg with the knee bent. Kick the foot forward to hit with the heel. The foot will move in a curve from inside to outside, and the foot will angle out. This kick is very important in **karate-jitsu**. It is used to attack the knee and the inside of the leg.

USING THE INSIDE KICK:

1. An attacker grabs you with his right hand.

2. Grab his right shoulder with your left hand.

3-5. Pull his shoulder as you kick his left leg at Sp-10.

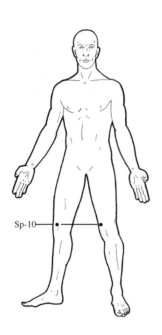

SIDE KICK *(YOKO-GERI)*:

Bend your leg and raise your knee. Then, drive your foot to the side. Hit with the bottom of the foot.

USING THE SIDE KICK:

1. An attacker grabs your left wrist.

2. Step slightly to your right as if to pull away.

3-4. With your left foot, kick the crease of his leg at point Sp-12.

A. You may also aim your kick at the Ki-center.

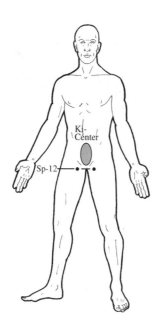

Martial Arts Morality: If someone has attacked you by grabbing your arm, you should not kick them unless: 1) You believe the grab is to be followed by a harmful attack, or 2) Your attacker is larger and stronger than you, so that you are out-matched.

KNEE STRIKE (*HIZA-GERI*):

Lift your knee up strongly and sharply. In essence, every kick begins with a knee strike because the very first motion of every kick is to bend and raise the knee. You could say that a kick is just a knee strike that was too far away [1-3].

USING THE KNEE STRIKE:

Pull your attacker down with your hands as you strike up with your knee. The best targets for knee strikes are the inside or outside of the leg, or the chest. [4]

"Here's an idea: You can use different parts of a kick, not just the end of the move. In this picture, George Dillman uses the recoil of a kick to catch an attacker's kick."

Chris Vitro practices self defense against an adult attacker (Will Skaggs), under the watchful eye of Bob "Bit Bull" Golden.

CHAPTER SIX: Defense Against Adults (*GOSHIN-WAZA*)

Karate-do is children's karate. It proves that young people can learn a lot from doing karate. **Karate-jitsu** helps people the same way. But, in **karate-jitsu** young people also learn self-defense that they can use.

The following self-defense moves work against adults. These moves *really work*, but don't think that they will make you a super fighter. Even the very best lose sometimes. Even the very best can be beaten. So, you must surprise your attacker. If he knows you are going to fight back, he will just throw you down and sit on you.

Practice these moves on someone. Learn to do them quickly and smoothly. In the pictures we show them 1-2-3. In real life they are done as one action.

SELF-DEFENSE MOVE # 1

1. An adult has his right hand on your shoulder and is reaching to touch you with his left.

2-4. With your right hand, grab the little finger of his left hand. With your left hand, grab his wrist and squeeze your fingers into the pressure point H-6 on his wrist.

5. With your right hand, bend his little finger back and twist it in. With your left hand, pull his wrist towards your body.

6. Push down with both hands to throw him to the ground. Then, run away as fast as you can.

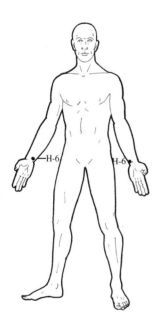

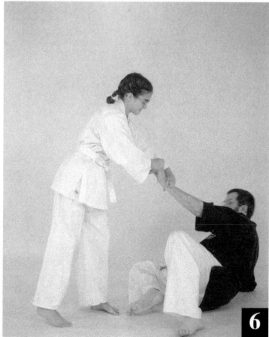

SELF-DEFENSE MOVE # 2

1. An adult has grabbed you by the arms, above your elbows.

2. Press your right hand on top of his right hand. This is to keep his hand on your arm as you move.

3-4. Kick his left leg at Sp-10 with a right inside kick.

5. After you kick, step forward and roll your left arm over his right arm. This turns his wrist over.

6. Press down with your left arm on his arm at SI-7. He will be in great pain and will fall down so you can run away.

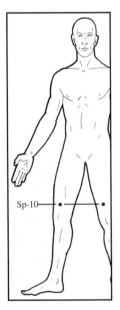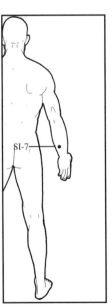

SELF-DEFENSE MOVE # 3
This move is almost the same as # 2.

1. An adult grabs you by both wrists. (Your fingers are up.)

2. Put your right hand on the back of his right hand to pin it to your left arm.

3-4. Kick his left leg at Sp-10 with a right inside kick.

5-6. Roll your left forearm over his right arm at SI-7, turning his wrist. Step forward and use your weight to press down with your left forearm on his arm. This will drop him to the floor so you can run away.

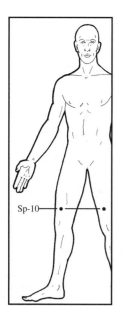
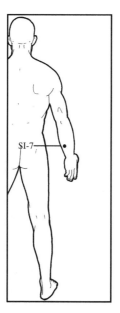

NOTE: *Be careful that your left arm is on top of his right arm, and does not roll over it.*

SELF-DEFENSE MOVE # 4

1. An adult grabs you by both wrists. (Your fingers are down.)

2. Swing your hands out.

3-4. Swing your hands in. Bring your right hand close to the base of your chest bone. (You are very strong with your hands like this.) Swing your left arm up as high as your shoulders.

"Be sure to do all of the steps as one smooth action. If you do 1, then 2, then 3, and so on, it will not work."

(Continued)

5. Smash down with your left arm. You are trying to smash the knuckles of his right hand down onto his left wrist. You make him hit himself at pressure point L-8.

6. Shoot your right hand up towards his face. *(This pulls your hand out of his grasp.)*

7-8. Punch the soft part under his chin with the knuckle of your middle finger. *[See Diagram]*

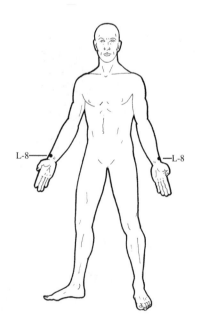

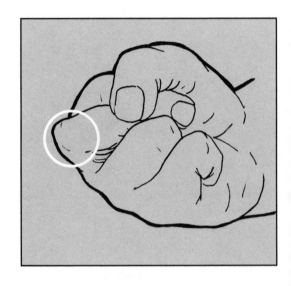

9. Smash your right wrist down on point L-8 on the attacker's right wrist. This will free your left hand.

10-11. Kick the inside of his leg at Sp-10 with your right foot.

12. Run away.

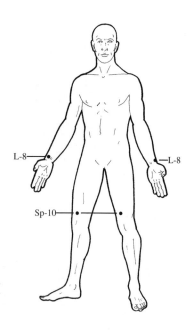

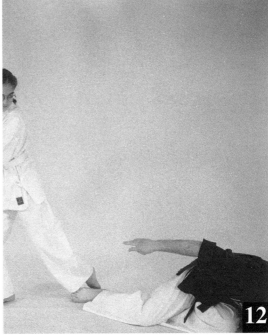

SELF-DEFENSE MOVE # 5

1. An attacker grabs your left arm with both hands and will not let you go.

2. Step forward slightly with your left foot, and bend your left arm. Bring your hand near the base of your chest bone where you are strong.

3-4. Roll your left fist up and forward. This crosses up his arms. If you look carefully, you will see that you have just done a basic middle counter.

5. Turn your left hand over and grab his left wrist at H-6 & L-8.

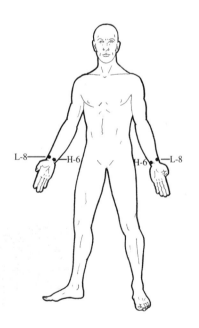

2

"Even though he can keep you from pulling free, he cannot keep you from bending your own elbow. This is an important secret of self-defense."

4

5

6-8. Kick your attacker's left leg at Sp-10 with a right inside kick. This will sprawl him out and bring his head down.

9-10. Grab his hair with your right hand and make a small circle with his head. Then, pull his head close to your hip.

11. Smash upward into your attacker's face with your left knee. Then, push him away and run.

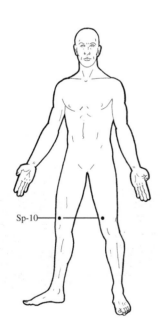

Bruce Lee was reading a martial arts magazine when he came upon an article about pressure points and their use in fighting. He became so excited that he forgot the difference in time zones and called George Dillman on the phone. "This is it!" He told Dillman. Dillman answered, "Bruce, it's the middle of the night!"

When Dillman thinks back on moments like that today, he can't help but wonder if he was destined to teach **kyusho-jitsu**.

"A lifetime of study in the martial arts helps to keep you strong and healthy."
-- George Dillman

CHAPTER SEVEN: Training Methods
(HOJO UNDO)

In this chapter, we show a drill that helps with eye-hand coordination. (Eye-hand coordination is what you need to catch a baton, or hit a pitch.) We also show a drill taught to George Dillman by **Bruce Lee**. This will help make your hands very fast.

MIRROR DRILL # 1

1. You and your friend stand about six feet apart. Your friend will throw punches or kicks your way. But, your friend will not come close to you. You do not touch each other in this drill.

2. If your friend punches with his right hand, you will bring up your left arm.

3. When your friend punches with his left arm, bring up your right arm.

4. If your friend kicks with his right leg, bring up your left leg.

5. When your friend kicks with his left leg, bring up your right leg.

6-7. When you make a mistake, correct it right away. So, if your friend punches with his right hand and you bring up your right hand, bring up your left hand as fast as you can.

"To help you with this drill, watch your friend's eyes. When you watch his eyes, you can still see his whole body. Also, his eyes can tell you what he is going to do. You may see him looking to aim his attack. Where he looks is where you have to cover."

MIRROR DRILL # 2

As you get good at the first mirror drill, try this one. Have your friend throw two attacks. You will do two covers and then an attack of your own.

EXAMPLE 1

1. Your friend punches with his right arm, and you bring up your left arm.

2. Your friend kicks with his right leg. You lift your left leg.

3. Keep your left leg up, and kick.

EXAMPLE 2

4. Your friend kicks with his right leg. You lift your left leg.

5. Your friend punches with his right arm. You lift your left arm.

6. You punch with your right arm.

MARTIAL ARTS LEGENDS: The late Danny Pai, whose legacy continues in Pai Lum kung fu. The late Bruce Lee, whose legacy continues in his movies and in his Jeet Kune Do system. Jhoon Rhee, "the Father of U.S. Tae Kwon Do." George Dillman, pressure point expert.

BRUCE LEE'S FAST-HANDS DRILL

If you want to punch hard, you will not be quick. If you want to be quick, your punch will not hit very hard. This is nature. In **karate-jitsu** *we use both quick and hard punches. Quick punches can "soften up" an attacker. Hard punches can end an attacker's assault. This drill helps to make punches quick.* **Bruce Lee** *taught this to* **George Dillman**.

1. Hold your right fist out as if you have punched.

2-3. Bend your elbow and snap your fist back. Make your fist touch your shoulder.

Next try to shoot your punch out and snap it back very fast. It will be like a whip.

4. Start with your elbow bent and your fist near your shoulder.

5-6. Punch forward as quickly as you can, then snap your fist back without any pause.

7-8. Try to touch your fist to your shoulder.

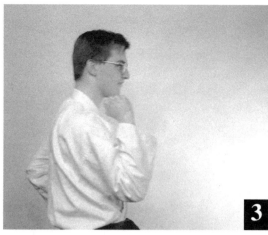

George Dillman worked with Muhammad Ali for three years in the early 70's. During this time, Dillman showed Ali karate concepts and how they could be applied to boxing. They also did road-work together, and Ali worked on defending not only punches, but also kicks. And Dillman occasionally served as Ali's body-guard.

There is a custom of presenting an honorary black belt to a person who helps promote and further karate, even though they do not practice the art. Dillman had given former Vice President Hubert Humphrey such a promotion. But, he awarded Muhammad Ali a regular black belt rank. When people asked him about this, his answer was, "You spar with Ali, then tell me he doesn't deserve a black belt."

In fact, Muhammad Ali was quite proficient at karate style sparring, and made it a point to spar with -- and beat -- black belt students Dillman brought to Ali's training camp. "Bruce Lee taught me *how* to be fast," says Dillman. "But it was Ali who *made* me fast. I mean, you had to be fast because he was so quick."

ABOVE: George Dillman and Muhammad Ali train together in the wooded areas around Ali's training camp, in Deer Lake, PA.

BELOW: Ali and Kim Dillman enjoy an impromptu sparring session.

> " **A**lways show respect for your teacher, your fellow karate students, and your family. "

At the beginning of a karate class, students kneel to meditate and pay their respects to their teacher and their art. -- Photo of **Bob Golden's School of Self Defense**

CHAPTER EIGHT: Form Training (KATA)

The most important part of karate is **kata**. A kata is a step by step set of karate moves. Long ago, karate masters created the kata using their best secrets. There are many of these kata which have been handed down for years and years.

Some kata are short, with only 10-20 steps. Other kata are long and have over 100. By doing the kata for a long time, karate students try to learn the secrets of the masters. And every secret can be found in kata. All of the basic moves you have seen so far can be found in various kata. The self-defense moves we have shown are all taken from kata, and, all the secrets of pressure points are hidden in the kata.

On the following pages we show a kata called **Pinan Nidan** (sounds like *peen-yawn knee-dawn*). When you look at the kata, you will see moves that you have learned. You will see horse stance, front stance and cat stance. You will see upward counter, downward counter, and step punch. There are also moves you have not seen yet, like hammer fist and downward knife hand counter.

It would be easy for you to look at this kata and imagine that it was just a kind of dance, or that it was just a fancy way to do your basic moves. But it is actually full of deep knowledge. It would take us many books to write down everything in this one kata.

When you do kata, you must do it with your mind as well as your body. See your attacker in your mind as you practice. Imagine yourself using your basic moves just as we have shown. This is the first step to learning advanced karate.

PINAN NIDAN

OPENING
1-2. Stand with your heels together, toes angled outward, and bow.

MOVE # 1
3. Bring both hands up to shoulder height, and place the back of your right fist against the palm of your left hand.

4. Draw your hands in towards your body, then press them down and forward in front of your belly. At the same time, pull your feet together and raise your big toes.

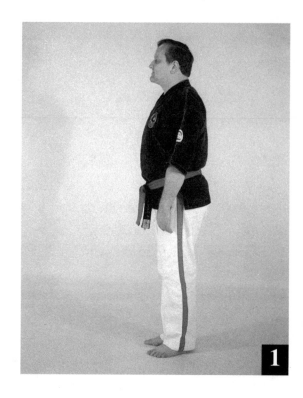

MOVE # 2

5. Draw both fists to your hips.

6. Step to the right so your feet are as wide as your shoulders.

7. Shoot your fists out in front of your belly.

MOVE # 3

8-9. Step to your left into a horse stance and do a left downward counter.

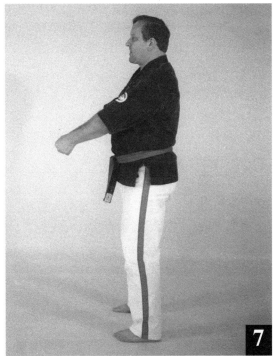

MOVE # 4

10-12. Pull your left foot back and take a cat stance. Swing your left arm over your head, then hammer down with your fist.

MOVE # 5

13. Step forward and do a step-punch with your right fist.

MOVE # 6

14-15. Step back with your right foot into a horse stance and do a right downward counter.

MOVE # 7

16. Pull your right foot back and take a cat stance. Swing your right arm over your head, then hammer down with your fist.

MOVE # 8

17. Step forward and do a step-punch with your left fist.

MOVE # 9

18-19. Step your left foot to the left, and turn into a left front stance. Do a left downward counter.

MOVE # 10

20-21. Step forward and do a right upward counter.

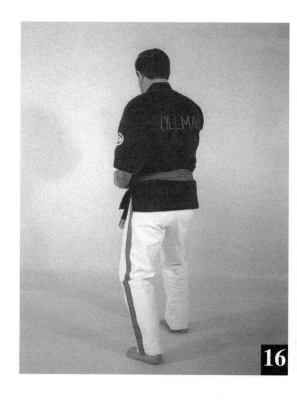

MOVE # 11
22. Step forward and do a left upward counter.

MOVE # 12
23. Step forward and do a right upward counter.

MOVE # 13
24-25. Swing your left foot behind you. Then turn around to face the back corner. Take a left front stance and do a left downward counter.

MOVE # 14
26. Step toward the back corner and do a right step-punch at neck level.

MOVE # 15
27-28. Swing your right foot to the right. Turn and take a right front stance facing the other back corner. Do a right downward counter.

MOVE # 16
29. Step toward the back corner and do a left step-punch at neck level.

MOVE # 17
30-31. Swing your left foot to the left. Turn to face the rear in left front stance, and do a left downward counter.

MOVE # 18
32. Step forward and do a right step-punch.

MOVE # 19

33. Step forward and do a left straight punch.

MOVE # 20

34. Step forward with a strong shout (kiai) and do a right step-punch.

MOVE # 21

35-36. Swing your left leg behind you to the right. Turn to face the front corner and take a left cat stance. Do a left knife hand downward counter.

MOVE # 22

37-38. Step toward the front corner into a right cat stance. Do a right knife hand downward counter.

MOVE # 23

39-40. Swing your right leg to the right. Turn to face the other front corner and take a right cat stance. Do a right knife hand downward counter.

MOVE # 24

41-42. Step toward the corner into a left cat stance. Do a left knife hand downward counter.

MOVE # 25

43. Draw the left foot back, and stand with your feet as wide as your shoulders, facing front. At the same time, draw your fists to your hips.

44. Shoot your fists out in front of your belly.

MOVE # 26

45. Bring your right foot next to the left foot and stand with your heels together, toes angled outward. Bring both hands up to shoulder height, and place the back of your right fist against the palm of your left hand.

46. Draw your hands in towards your body, then press them down and forward in front of your belly. At the same time, pull your feet together and raise your big toes.

CLOSING

47-48. Let your hands hang at your sides, and bow.

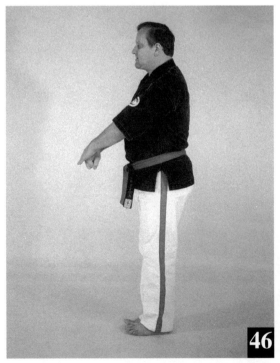

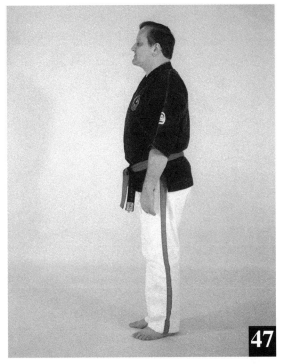

FRONT VIEWS

The following pictures show moves 2-6 from the front.

MOVE # 2
A. Stand so your feet are as wide as your shoulders. Shoot your fists out in front of your belly.

MOVE # 3
B-C. Step to your left into a horse stance and do a left downward counter.

MOVE # 4
D-F. Pull your left foot back and take a cat stance. Swing your left arm over your head, then hammer down with your fist.

FRONT VIEWS (Continued)

MOVE # 5
G-H. Step forward and do a step-punch with your right fist.

MOVE # 6
I-J. Step back with your right foot into a horse stance and do a right downward counter.

PINAN NIDAN

 **3a**
 **3b**
 **4a**
 **4b**
 **4c**

 **9a**
 **9b**
 **10**
 **11**
 **12**

 **16**
 **17a**
 **17b**
 **18**
 **19**

 **23a**
 **23b**
 **24a**
 **24b**
 **25a**

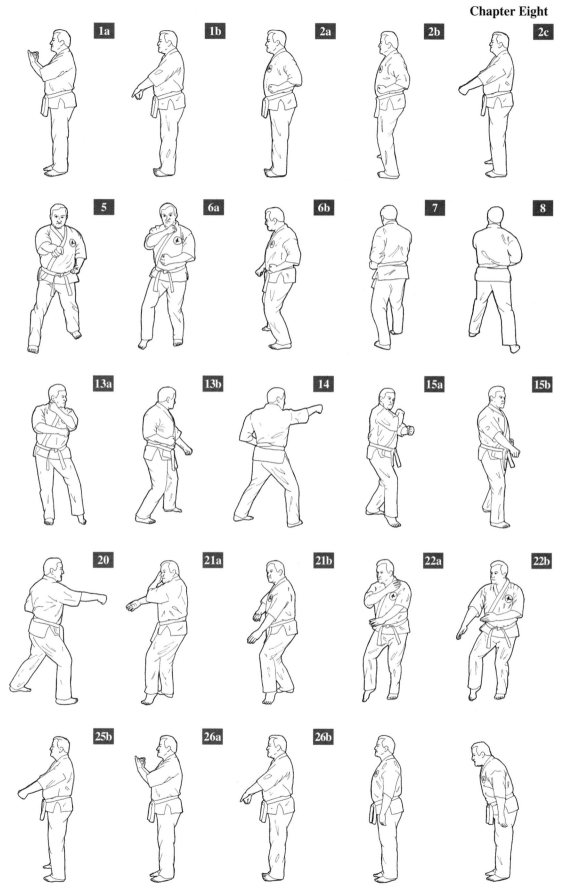

HOW TO PRACTICE KATA

When learning the children's **karate-do**, the most important thing is to do what you are told. "Don't think, don't ask questions, just do." This is what **karate-do** teachers have said. So, in **karate-do** the goal of kata training is to learn to do the kata exactly as you are told to do it.

However, in **karate-jitsu** the most important thing is knowing what each kata move is used for. The use of the moves in a kata is called **bunkai** (sounds like *boon-kai*). Bunkai begins in your imagination when you do kata and picture yourself using each move. Then, you should practice the bunkai with a partner. The next time you do the kata, you will remember how it felt working with a real person, and that will help you imagine the bunkai more vividly.

When you perform the step punches in Pinan Nidan, imagine that you are pinning an attacker's foot to the floor as you hit. When you perform the downward counters, imagine you have caught an attacker's finger and you are putting him on the ground. When you do the rising counters, see yourself being attacked by someone who grabs you and is about to hit you in the face. Picture yourself hitting down on his arm, then driving your forearm up under his jaw. Every time you do the kata, picture everything you know about each move as you do that move.

On the next pages you will see an example of bunkai. Here we show a use for moves # 7 and # 8. This is not the only way you can apply these steps. If you use your imagination, you may be able to come up with other ideas for bunkai.

"As you do the kata, picture how you would use each move."

BUNKAI from Pinan Nidan

1. An attacker grabs your right arm near the elbow with his right hand.

2. Swing your right fist up and trap his hand in the bend of your elbow.

3. Turn slightly to your right and take a cat stance. This puts pressure on the attacker's wrist and turns his body away.

(Notice that this is like the use for middle counter which we showed earlier. The swinging of your right hand and the turning of your body is the first part of move # 7 in Pinan Nidan [A,B,C].)

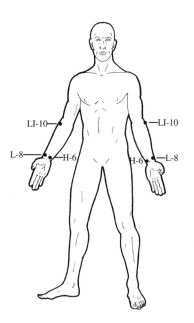

BUNKAI from Pinan Nidan (Cont.)

4. Strike down on the attacker's right arm. Hit him on pressure point LI-10 on the outside of his forearm with the knuckle of your little finger. *(This action completes move # 7 of the kata [D].)*

5. Step forward with your left foot.

6. Step on your attacker's toes with your left foot to pin him in place. Grab his right wrist on pressure points H-6 and L-8 with your right hand. Then, pull his right hand sharply to your right hip, while you hit him with your left punch. *(This is kata move # 8 [E,F].)*

Note: Pressure point targets on the body are described in ***Advanced Pressure Point Fighting of RYUKYU KEMPO.***

H ere is another example of bunkai for kata moves # 15 & 16, which George Dillman taught during a seminar at Bill Burch's school. As an attacker reaches with his right hand, catch his fingers with your right hand (1). Turn your body 45 degrees to the right, as you use a downward counter to send the attacker to the floor (2,3). Take a short step forward and strike with your left fist to a pressure point on his head (4).

Need more ideas for bunkai? Compare kata movement # 4 with the position that George Dillman is in on page 17.

CONCLUSION

In less than 100 years the secret art of karate has spread all over the world. Today it is practiced by people of all ages, children, youths, adults and even grandparents. But, it has circled the globe as the children's art of **karate-do**. The old combat art of **karate-jitsu** is just starting to become known again.

In this book we have shown the basic moves of **karate-jitsu**. More importantly, we have shown how to use the moves properly. It is the use of the moves which makes the real difference between **karate-jitsu** and **karate-do**. And, it is the pressure points which make the difference between moves that work in real self-defense and moves that only look good on paper.

Though this book is small, the information in it is more than some black belts possess. But do not feel smug. This book barely begins to touch on the deep secrets of the art of **karate-jitsu**. We, the authors, have studied for decades, and we are still learning more and more. There is a lifetime of study ahead for you, too.

Here is our last word of advice to you in your training: Use your imagination, ask good questions and never stop learning. It is our hope that the old art of **karate-jitsu** will know a strong future in you.

APPENDIX ONE: The Karate Belt

Karate-ka (karate students) wear a belt called an **obi**. The color of the belt tells the rank in karate. Ranks below black belt are called **kyu**. Black belt ranks are called **dan**. It takes 3 to 5 years to reach black belt.

RANK	BELT COLOR	TOTAL TRAINING
(KYU RANK)		
9th kyu (ku-kyu)	white	3 months
8th kyu (hachi-kyu)	white (one green stripe)	6 months
7th kyu (shichi-kyu)	yellow	9 months
6th kyu (roku-kyu)	blue	1 year
5th kyu (go-kyu)	green	1 1/4 years
4th kyu (yon-kyu)	purple	1 3/4 years
3rd kyu (san-kyu)	brown	2 years
2nd kyu (ni-kyu)	brown (one black stripe)	2 1/2 years
1st kyu (ik-kyu)	brown (two black stripes)	3 years
(DAN RANK)		
1st dan (shodan)	black	3-5 years
2nd dan (nidan)	black	7 years
	(at least 2 years after shodan)	
(INSTRUCTOR RANK)		
3rd dan (sandan)	black	10 years
	(2-3 years after nidan)	
(MASTER RANK)		
4th dan (yondan)	black & red	15 years
5th dan (godan)	black & red	20 years
6th dan (rokudan)	black & red	25 years
(GRANDMASTER RANK)		
7th dan (shichidan)	red & black	30 years
8th dan (hachidan)	red & black	over 35 years
9th dan (kudan)	red & black	over 40 years
(HEADMASTER)		
10th dan (judan)	red	over 50 years

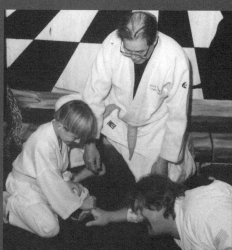

APPENDIX TWO: Glossary of Terms

AGE-UKE: *(ah-gay oo-kay)* "Upward Counter." A counter move, so-named because the arm sweeps up, in front of the face.

BUJITSU: *(boo-jit-soo)* "Warrior Fighting Arts." The combat science of the Japanese Samurai.

BUNKAI: *(boon-kai)* "Application." The use of karate moves in real self-defense.

CHUAN FA: *(chwan fah)* "Fist Method." Chinese boxing, which is called "kung fu" by most people.

CHUDAN-UKE: *(chew-dahn oo-kay)* "Middle counter." A counter move, so-named because the arm sweeps across at the level of the body.

DACHI: *(dah-chee)* ."Stance." Special ways of standing used in karate.

DAN: *(dahn)* "Level." Levels of black belt.

GEDAN-UKE: *(gay-dahn oo-kay)* "Lower counter." Downward counter, so named because the arm sweeps down across the lower part of the body.

GOSHIN: *(go-sheen)* "Self-defense."

GYAKU-ZUKI: *(gyah-koo zoo-kee)* "Reverse punch." To punch with the rear hand. So, if your right foot is forward, the rear hand is the left.

HOJO-UNDO: *(hoe-joe oon-doe)* "Training Methods." Drills and exercises to improve strength, speed or other skills needed in karate.

KARATE-DO: *(kah-rah-tay-doe)* "Way of the Empty Hand." An art created for teaching school-children based on Okinawan fighting methods.

KARATE-JITSU: *(kah-rah-tay-jit-soo)* "Chinese Hand Fighting." An Okinawan method of self-defense based on Chinese kung fu, Japanese bujitsu, and Okinawan te. Can also be pronounced tode-jitsu (toe-day-jit-soo), or toudi-jitsu (too-dee-jit-soo).

KARATE-KA: *(kah-rah-tay-kah)* "Karate-ist." A person who does karate.

KATA: *(kah-tah)* "Form." Formal set pattern of movements.

KEMPO: *(kem-poe)* "Fist Method." The Okinawan way of saying "Chuan fa" (kung fu). Sometimes written Kenpo.

KERI-WAZA: *(kay-ree wah-zah)* "Kicking Techniques."

KI: *(kee)* "Vital energy." The word ki can mean breath, spirit, energy, and more. A good way to understand this is "life force."

KIAI: *(kee-eye)* "Uniting the spirit." The strong shout used by karate experts to strengthen their techniques.

KIBA-DACHI: *(kee-bah dah-chee)* "Horse Stance." To stand with the feet apart as if riding a horse.

KIHON: *(kee-hone)* "Basic." The basic moves of karate.

KUNG FU: *(kung foo)* "Skill." Any skill gained by hard work, but usually referring to Chinese martial arts.

KYU: (kyoo) "Grade." A level of skill below black belt.

KYUSHO-JITSU: *(cue-show-jit-soo)* "Pressure Point Fighting." The science of using pressure points for self-defense.

MAE-GERI: *(may gay-ree)* "Front Kick." A kick to the front with the ball of the foot.

NAIHANCHI-GERI: *(nye-hahn-chee gay-ree)* "Naihanchi Kick." Inside kick. Named Naihanchi-geri because it is used in a kata called Naihanchi.

NEKO-DACHI: *(nay-koe dah-chee)* "Cat Stance." To stand with most of your weight on your back leg, and your front foot just touching the floor.

OBI: *(oh-bee)* "Belt." The colored belt used to show a person's level of skill in karate.

OI-ZUKI: *(oy-zoo-kee)* "Step Punch." To step forward and punch.

PINAN NIDAN: *(peen-yahn nee-dahn)* "Peaceful, Second Level." The second of five fundamental kata common to many styles of karate.

RYUKYU KEMPO: *(ryoo-kyoo kem-poe)* "Okinawan Fist Method." An old name for karate. Ryukyu is another name for Okinawa.

SHUTO-UKE: *(shoo-toe oo-kay)* "Knife Hand Counter." A counter move, so named because the edge of the open hand is used to deliver a cutting or chopping blow.

TE: *(tay)* "Hand." An Okinawan fighting art used by royal bodyguards.

TOMARI-TE: *(toe-mar-ee-tay)* "Hands of Tomari." The kind of karate that comes from the village of Tomari.

TSUKI: *(tsoo-kee)* "Thrust." A punch. In the Japanese language there is no word for punch. Instead the word tsuki is used for any kind of poking, stabbing or thrusting action.

UKE: *(oo-kay)* "Receive." Counter moves used to stop an attacker.

WAZA: *(wah-zah)* "Technique." The fighting moves of karate.

YOKO-GERI: *(yoe-koe gay-ree)* "Side kick." A kick to the side with the bottom of the foot.

YUDANSHA: *(yoo-dahn-shah)* "Dan-holder." A black belt.

ZENKUTSU-DACHI: *(zen-koot-soo dah-chee)* "Front stance." To stand with one leg in front and your weight forward.

COUNTING:
    1 = Ichi: *(ee-chee)*
    2 = Ni: *(nee)*
    3 = San: *(sahn)*
    4 = Shi: *(shee)* or sometimes Yon *(Yone)*
    5 = Go
    6 = Roku: *(roe-koo)*
    7 = Shichi: *(shee-chee)*
    8 = Hachi: *(hah-chee)*
    9 = Ku: *(koo)*
    10 = Ju: *(joo)*
    11 = Ju-ichi
    12 = Ju-ni
    20 = Ni-ju
    21 = Ni-ju-ichi
    30 = San-ju
    100 = Ha-ku

"Some people say, Practice makes perfect. They're wrong. Practice makes permanent; perfect practice makes perfect."

Instructional Videos from
DILLMAN KARATE INTERNATIONAL

Tape #5: George Dillman's Theory on Healing
Tape teaches "Energy Restoration," "Head Revival," pain dissipation, energy theory and other concepts vital to the safe practice of kyusho-jitsu.

Tape #6: Naihanchi
Tape teaches pressure point theory and method. Contains complete instruction on performing the kata Naihanchi, as well as a thorough breakdown of the moves for real self-defense.

Tapes #5 & #6 are the essential video companions to the pressure point instructional books written by George Dillman and Chris Thomas.

Tape #D Okinawan Traditional Weapons
In this tape, Grandmaster George Dillman teaches traditional karate weapons, with special emphasis on the bo (six-foot staff). Includes bo kata.

Tape #F Go with the Flow: a Seminar with Grandmaster George Dillman, Professor Remy Presas and Professor Wally Jay.
Tape contains instruction from three of the world's most famous and sought-after martial arts teachers. See what makes a master, and learn how different arts can compliment each other.

For information and pricing for these, and other videos and books, send SASE to:

Dillman Karate International
251 Mt. View Rd.
Reading, PA 19607-9744 USA

Over 30 Titles Available.